MY PARENTS ARE SL AND I AM WHOLE!

by

Andrea Seydel

Coloured by Felicia Fleetwood

"Children and adults will love this positive, empowering book. My parents are separated and I am whole, is a powerful tool for teaching children to think positive. The affirmations in this book help children develop and practice the core building blocks of constructive internal dialogue and positive self talk."

-Andrea Seydel Positive Psychology Practitioner

MY PARENTS ARE SEPARATED AND I AM WHOLE!

Andrea Seydel Coloured by Felicia Fleetwood
Live Life Happy Publishing Inc.

Library of Congress Cataloging in Publication data
Seydel, Andrea
My parents are separated and I am whole / Andrea Seydel
ISBN
1. Self-actualization (Psychology)-Teaching (Early Childhood) 2. Life Skills- Study and Learning (Early childhood)
3. Self Help-Childhood
ISBN-13: 978-1515269168
1st Printing September 2015. Printed in Canada
Cover and interior design by Andrea Seydel
Edited by Carole Seydel

Publisher's Note & DISCLAIMER
This publication is designed to provide support and guided affirmations concerning the subject matter covered. It is sold with the understanding that the publisher and author are not engaging in or rendering any psychological, medical or other professional services. This book by no means replaces medical attention or professional care. Please seek medical professional support if you require.

Live Life Happy Publishing
www.andreaseydel.com | 416-456-7555

Dedication

To my children!
Damian and Felicia,
your happiness
carries me!

ACKNOWLEDGEMENTS

This book is dedicated to my kids, Damian and Felicia, my little cuties. I love and care for you both beyond words. This book was created for you during a time when you both proved to be strong! I wish I could erase all hurt and hope I made the transition of separation as positive and smooth as possible for you. Thank you for trusting and loving me.

To my parents for instilling in me the skills to see a positive outlook on life and for teaching me how to see the light in every situation. Thank you for your unconditional love. To you, the parents, for being brave and supportive of your children during a time of change in your family!

My parents live in separate homes and I am okay!

My parents are both special to me. My parents both love me very much. I am lovable!

I am grateful for my parents. My parents will always be available for me. I am okay!

My parents separating allows for new possibilities. I have double the opportunities. Life goes on to bright happy days. I am happy!

I am confident. I see the world filled with new possibilities. I am excited! I am lucky!

I am loved and my life is filled with good things. Life is fun!

I am surrounded and loved by many people. I am loved!

Things work out for me.
I know I am safe at all times.
Life is good!

The world is a safe and gentle place. People care about me, and I care about people. I feel loved!

I am thankful for all the love around me. I have friends and family that love and support me.

I talk out my feelings peacefully. My feelings guide me, I listen to them, and I express them. I am ok!

I let go of hurt and start fresh.
I am okay with tears
and expressing my feelings.
I feel good!

Set backs only make me a stronger person. I am a strong!

My family and friends listen and support me. I feel calm and relaxed!

I love myself and I am a beautiful person. I am love-able!

The decisions of others may affect me, but I am not at fault. I deserve love and patience. I am a wonderful person filled with love!

My parents support and assure me of love daily. I deserve kindness and thoughtful attention. I am whole, complete and perfect just as I am!

I can see the good things in my life. I believe in myself and my abilities. I am brave!

I choose to be happy. I am full of joy, happiness and love. Things work out well for me!

My parents are separated
and I am whole!

ABOUT THE AUTHOR

Andrea Seydel is a mother of two children and has been through a separation/divorce. She received her B.A. in Psychology from York University, with post graduate studies in Counselling Psychology and is a Positive Psychology Practitioner. As a Life Coach, Fitness & Yoga instructor she is always encouraging her clients and participants to stay positive and enjoy life's blessings, Andrea was not going to let a separation negatively affect her kids. My Parents are Separated and I am Whole, was designed to help her children stay positive through a changing time, and now it is here for you as well. Andrea's passion to help others recognize and tap into their potential to live their best life is seen in her counselling, books, classes, and seminars. Her enthusiasm and passion, combined with her health and positive psychology knowledge make self improvement almost contagious. She loves to spend her time hiking the trails with her rescue dogs, doing yoga and having fun times with her family in Caledon, Ontario.

ABOUT THE ILLUSTRATOR

Felicia Fleetwood is an energetic eight year old girl, who takes her learning very seriously. She loves to read and surround herself with countless books. She approaches every task with a positive attitude. Felicia is a creative spirit and has enjoyed art classes since she was very young. When she offered to colour the pictures for this book, her mom couldn't say NO. Felicia at random likes to make art creations and write letters of love and appreciation. Felicia says from this book and going through her parents' separation, she learned how to persevere and make an effort to respond positively to challenges. She said reading and hearing loving positive statements regularly, made her feel happy and loved. Felicia loves dancing and wishes she could rescue more dogs!

Made in the USA
Middletown, DE
16 July 2017